TASMANIA

TASMANIA

THE BEAUTIFUL ISLAND

NEW HOLLAND

INTRODUCTION

Tasmania is an island state of Australia, located 240 kilometres to the south of the mainland, and is renowned for its breathtaking natural scenery.

With a reputation as a foodie's paradise, Tasmania is famous for its gourmet cuisine, including cheese, apple cider, wine, and beer, made from locally sourced ingredients. The island boasts a wide range of fresh seafood, including the famous Tassie Scallop Pie, which can be found at most bakeries.

Tasmania is home to five out of the 11 UNESCO World Heritage-listed convict sites in Australia, as well as some of the world's most beautiful white sandy beaches and spectacular coastlines.

Visitors can enjoy the sight of pods of dolphins, migrating whales, and seabirds, including albatrosses, falcons, and sea eagles, as well as a variety of native animals such as the Tasmanian Devil, which is unique to the island.

Tasmania is also home to the world's most ancient and tallest trees, as well as Mount Ossa, the highest mountain in the state, standing at 1617 metres.

Visitors can witness the Southern Lights all year round, with some months offering longer and darker nights for better viewing opportunities.

With its unique and special wildlife, rich history, incredible produce and ingredients, and a balanced lifestyle, Tasmania is one of the most desirable and popular destinations in Australia.

THE CITIES

Hobart.

MÖVENPICK

Hobart Waterfront & Salamanca.

Hobart Museum and Gallery.

Hobart's iconic Tasman Bridge.

Tasman Bridge with kunanyi/Mount Wellington.

Mawson's Huts Replica Museum in Hobart.

Museum of Old and New Art MONA situated at Berriedale Bay of river Derwent in Hobart.

Victoria Dock Hobart.

Sullivans Cove.

Salamanca street shopping precinct.

Salamanca Market.

Japanese garden inside of the Royal Tasmanian Botanical Gardens.

Hobart Town Hall.

Hobart's Parliament House.

Tasman Bridge.

MONA, Museum of Old and New Art, situated at Berriedale bay of river Derwent in Hobart.

MONA museum building.

Outdoor art installations at MONA.

MONA art museum.

KUNANYI / MOUNT WELLINGTON

Kunanyi / Mount Wellington, Tasmania's stunning natural attraction is located in the southeast of Tasmania. Mount Wellington is the summit of the Wellington Range and resides in the Wellington Park reserve. Hobart sits at the foot of the mountain.

Although the trail is challenging, taking an average of over 3 hours to complete, it is a popular destination for hiking and walking, so you are likely

to encounter other explorers. Open year-round, the area is beautiful to visit anytime.

The mountain has a remarkable impact on Hobart's weather. If you plan to visit the summit, be prepared for the chilly winds, as they can be quite icy. In winter, the summit is frequently snow-capped, while lighter snowfalls in spring, summer and autumn are a common occurrence. A day on the summit can vary from clear sunny skies to rain, snow, and icy winds, and back to clear conditions again.

Mount Wellington lookout in Hobart.

Mount wellington lookout.

Mount Wellington (Kunanyi)

The view overlooking Hobart from Mount Wellington.

Mount Wellington.

Mount Wellington.

Mount Wellington with snow.

Mount Wellington in Hobart a major tourist attraction for its unique landscape of rocks.

PORT ARTHUR

PORT ARTHUR

Discover the Rich History and Natural Beauty of Port Arthur Historical Site Located just 90 minutes outside of Hobart, the Port Arthur Historical Site is a must-see destination for those interested in Australia's colonial past and convict history.

This renowned site has hundreds of stories to tell, from its early days as a timber station in 1830 to its transformation into a penitentiary that housed countless convicts in harsh conditions.

The site's remote location made it nearly impossible for prisoners to escape, and the infamous dog line at Eagle Hawk Neck served as a deterrent for those who dared to try.

Despite its dark past, today the Port Arthur Historical Site is a beautiful location that offers a wide range of activities, including cruises, historic site day tours, and exploring the 30-plus buildings, ruins, restored houses, heritage gardens, galleries, museums and walking trails.

The site's location on the stunning Tasman Peninsula also offers breathtaking coastlines and natural wonders, including the Tessellated Pavement, a natural rock platform, Waterfall Bay, and the Remarkable Cave – a tunnel-shaped cave formed from years of crashing waves that created a wall of sandstone and a tunnel that stands today to be explored.

As a world heritage site, Port Arthur Historical Site has become a popular destination for tourists from all over the world.

The blowhole at Eagle Hawk Neck and the rich wildlife complete the picturesque landscape.

Experience the beauty and sadness of this unique location and explore one of Australia's most popular tourist destinations.

The UNESCO world heritage penitentiary is located on the Tasman Peninsula, Port Arthur.

The garden in Port Arthur historic site.

Port Arthur Prison Corridor.

Port Arthur.

Port Arthur village historic site.

Port Arthur village historic site.

Port Arthur.

Port Arthur Convict Museum Settlement.

Port Arthur Penal Colony.

The Church at Port Arthur Historic Site.

The Penitentiary. Constructed in 1843 as a flour mill and granary.

Port Arthur Government Cottage.

Views of the Paupers' Mess In Historic Port Arthur.

Port Arthur.

Port Arthur Convict Museum.

St David's Anglican Church at the Port Arthur Historic Site.

Devil's Kitchen.

Tasman Peninsula dolerite cliffs and arch.

Tasman Peninsula.

Tasmans arch.

Blowhole in Port Arthur.

Tasman Island and The Blade. Three Capes Walk.

Launeston.

BATMAN FAWKNER INN
EATING & DRINKING ESTABLISHMENT
SINCE 1822
39
Budget
ACCOMMODATION
PASTA RESISTANCE &
THE eatery
6334 3081
YORK TOWN SQ
eatery

Launceston town

Historical houses in center of Launceston.

Launceston town centre.

The Tamar Island boardwalk in Lanceston.

THE CATARACT GORGE

The Cataract Gorge is a must-visit destination in Launceston, Tasmania. This stunning river gorge, located only 1.5 km from the city centre, offers visitors an opportunity to immerse themselves in the beauty of nature.

One of the top things to do at the Cataract Gorge is to take a leisurely walk along its hiking trails. The walk can take up to 2–3 hours, depending on how slow or fast you want to take the trail.

The area is also home to some fantastic dining options. The Gorge Restaurant, located in the Cliff Grounds Reserve, offers an excellent lunch venue, while the Basin Cafe at the First Basin serves lighter meals.

For an unforgettable experience, take a Cataract Gorge boat trip leaving from Home Point Parade, taking you through the lower section of the South Esk River, offering a unique perspective of the gorge and its stunning surroundings.

You can also take the chairlift across the gorge and First Basin, with top speeds of one metre per second. The slower ride allows passengers to enjoy the breathtaking views for a longer time.

In conclusion, Cataract Gorge is a gem in Launceston that offers visitors a chance to escape and unwind in nature. Whether you're looking for a leisurely hike, a delicious meal, or a unique experience, the gorge has something for everyone.

Cataract Gorge Reserve.

Cataract Gorge, Launceston

Cataract Gorge, Launceston.

Cataract Gorge.

Cataract Gorge Toll House.

Liffey's Falls.

South Esk River in Cataract Gorge

The first basin at Cataract Gorge over South Esk River in Launceston.

Daffodil walk at Cataract Gorge Reserve.

Tourist ride on Gorge Scenic Chairlift in Launceston.

Cataract Gorge Reserve.

City park in Launceston.

Launceston.

Marina in Launceston.

Windmill, Launceston.

Queen Victoria Museum Inveresk and Art Gallery.

Launceston City Park Conservatorium.

Burnie.

Burnie town.

Waterfront in Burnie.

Guide Falls, Burnie.

Burgess Cove just 45 minutes outside of Burnie.

Blue hour over Burgess Cove.

SPIRIT OF TASMANIA

Spirit of Tasmania II

Mersey River, Devonport.

Devonport.

Ross Female Factory which was for female convicts in the penal colony.

THE ROSS FEMALE FACTORY

A historic site in Tasmania erected in 1833, the Ross Female Factory is a significant landmark in the town of Ross.

Originally constructed to house the convict chain gangs who built the Ross Bridge, the factory was later repurposed to serve as a probation station for female convicts and their infants from 1847 to 1854.

Today, the Ross Female Factory is a protected historic site. Although few remains are visible above ground, it is the most intact archaeological site of its kind in Australia.

Visitors can explore the Overseer's Cottage to view a model of the factory from 1851 and learn about the site's rich history. For those interested in delving deeper into Ross's heritage, the Ross Heritage Trail passes by the factory and is well worth exploring.

Ross is located about 78 km south of Launceston along the Midlands Highway, approximately an hour's drive away.

CRADLE MOUNTAIN

CRADLE MOUNTAIN

Cradle Mountain is located in the Cradle Mountain–Lake St. Clair National Park, at the northern border of northwest-central Tasmania, Australia.

This mountain, which features a lava basalt peak rising to 1,545 m, is situated on Tasmania's central plateau and spans 1,611 square kilometers.

The national park's abundant wildlife includes Tasmanian devils, quolls, platypus, echidna, wombats, and the ever-curious black currawong, making it a true nature lover's paradise.

The best time to visit Tasmania is during summer, which runs from December to February when the temperature is warm and dry.

The Cradle Mountain Hike is a 12 km return walk that takes an average of 5 to 8 hours to complete. This difficult hike, which covers an elevation of 747 m, is not about the distance but rather the challenging nature of the trail itself.

Dove Lake and Cradle Moutain.

Cradle Mountain.

Cradle Mountain

Dove Lake.

Cradle Mountain.

THE SOUTHERN LIGHTS

Witness the Enchanting Aurora Australis in Tasmania. For those seeking the elusive southern light show, Tasmania is undoubtedly the ideal destination to experience it.

The Aurora Australis is a celestial event that is fleeting and can be challenging to capture. While images of green beams and purple glows are not typical, they can be transformed into a burst of colour.

This thrill of the hunt has turned thousands of Tasmanians into avid aurora chasers. The months between March and September are the best times to witness the southern lights, with longer, darker nights.

The South Arm Peninsula and Cockle Creek on the southern tip of Tasmania are the most popular viewing spots for this amazing and beautiful light show.

However, the skies must be clear for optimal viewing, so be sure to check for Aurora Alerts.

Auroras rely on charged particles from the sun, so they won't appear every night.

Aurora Australis in Carlton Beach.

The Southern Lights.

THE BEAUTY

THE BEAUTY OF TASMANIA

The beauty of Tasmania's natural wonders and unique wildlife makes the beauty of Tasmania unparalleled, with breathtaking views around every corner.

Despite its size, you can experience a large portion of its natural wonders by taking a short trip outside Hobart.

Keep an eye out for the unique wildlife, such as the Tasmanian Devil and platypus, as you follow our guide to explore the stunning Tasmanian wilderness.

Undoubtedly, Tasmania's biggest draw is its extraordinary wildlife and dramatic scenery. Rugged mountains, cliffs, ancient rainforests, and white-sand bays will leave you in awe.

You can find 3,000-year-old endemic trees, tumbling waterfalls, and historic Aboriginal sites hidden amidst them.

Every part of Tasmania offers spectacular views and lookouts that showcase the island's stunning landscapes.

From the rolling hills of the northwest coast to the breathtaking waters of the east coast, you're sure to fall in love with this beautiful island state.

Nelson Falls.

Tessellated Pavement, Eaglehawk Neck.

The Gardens, Bay of Fires.

Bay of Fires.

Bay of Fires.

Lichen-covered boulders
at Bay of Fires.

Bay of Fires.

Bay of Fires.

King Island.

Wynyard.

Wineglass Bay, Freycinet National Park.

The Nut, Stanley.

Home Beach Sunset on Three Hummock Island.

Cape Bruny Island.

Honeymoon Bay, Freycinet Peninsula.

Freycinet National Park.

Cradle Mountain, Lake St Clair National Park, Central Highlands.

Sarah Island.

Deadmans Bay, South Coast.

Beerbarrel Beach

South Cape Bay.

Bruny Island.

Lion Rock on the south coast.

Cethana Lake.

Cradle Mountain

Dove Lake, Cradle Mountain.

Painted Cliffs on Maria Island National Park.

Raspins Beach Conservation Area reserve in Orford.

Beach huts in Hobart.

Boat Harbour Beach.

Squeaking Point.

Binalong Bay.

Binalong Bay.

The Neck, Bruny Island.

Wineglass Bay.

The Dock lookout on Flinders Island.

Cape Bruny.

Hazards Beach at Freycinet National Park.

Hawley Beach, Tasmania.

Lagoons Beach Conservation Area and the A3 Tasman Highway near the village of Scamander.

Georges Bay, St Helens.

Sawyer Bay.

Binalong Bay.

Eddystone Point Lighthouse, Mount William National Park.

Macquarie Harbour.

Eddystone Point Lighthouse.

Cape Bruny Lighthouse, Bruny Island.

Cape Tourville Lighthouse.

Historic Lighthouse at Eddystone Point, Bay of Fires.

Hell's Gate Lighthouse.

WILDLIFE

Wallaby.

Common Brushtail Possum.

Wombat.

Seals on rocks.

Peacock at Cataract Gorge Reserve, Launceston.

Green Rosella or Tasmanian rosella is native to Tasmania and Bass Strait islands.

Laughing Kookaburra.

Chestnut Teal.

Tiger Quoll.

Bettong.

Pygmy Possum.

Rainbow Lorikeets.

Oystercatchers.

Seafull flock.

Short-beaked Echidna.

Blotched Blue-tongue Lizard (*Tiliqua nigrolutea*).

Magpie.

Yellow-crested Cockatoo.

Australian Fur Seals.

Black-faced Cormorant (*Phalacrocorax fuscescens*).

A Black Currawong.

Little Penguin.

Pelican at Bay of Fires.

Honey Bee on Manuka flower.

Albatross.

Albatross.

Great Egret, Tamar Islands near Launceston.

Eastern Grey Kangaroos.

Willie-wagtail (*Rhipidura leucophrys*).

Green Rosella
(*Platycercus caledonicus*).

A pair of great cormorants (*Phalacrocorax carbo*), Bruny Island.

Pacific Gull nesting.

Black Swan.

New Holland Honeyeater (*Phylidonyris novaehollandiae*).

Azure Kingfisher.

Wombats.

Common Seadragon.

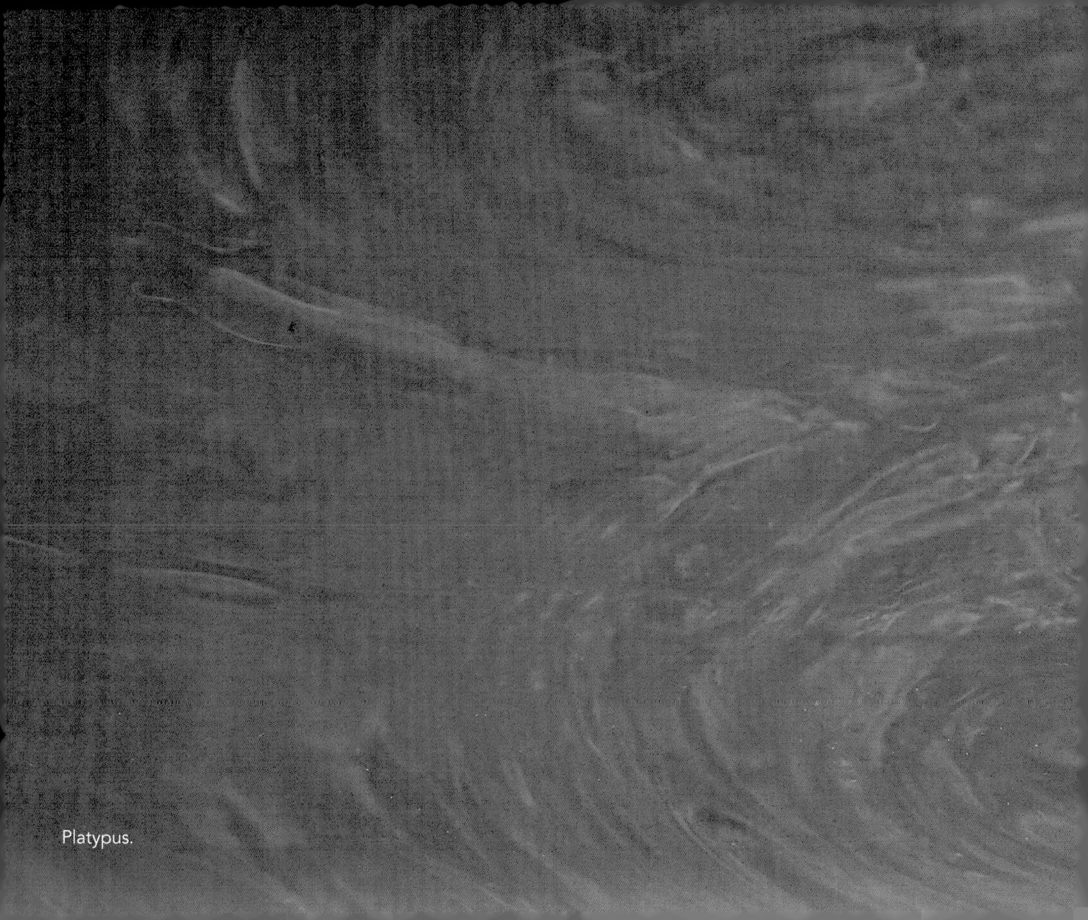

Platypus.

Tasmanian Devil.

Juvenile Tasmanian Devil.

Tasmanian Devil.

Spotted handfish, *Brachionichthys hirsutus* – one of the rarest fish.

Tasman Peninsula Underwater scenery of the Tasman Sea.

Dolphins jumping at Maria Island.

Seals in Abel Tasman
National Park.

Longsnout Boarfish,
Pentaceropsis recurvirostris.

Longsnout Boarfish, *Pentaceropsis recurvirostris*.

Humpback Whale.

Albino wallaby.

Mosaic Sugar Gliders.

NATURE

Tall Cheeseberry (*Cyathodes platystoma*) in southern Tasmania.

Grass Triggerplant, *Stylidium graminifolium*.

Epacris cerasicollina is a flowering plant endemic to Tasmania.

Tasmanian waratah, *Telopea truncata*.

Tasmanian Waratah (*Telopea truncata*).

Lavender farm near in the Tamar Valley.

Bellendena montana wildflowers.

Yellow Banksia flower.

Poppy field farm crop.

Pride of Madeira, (*Echium candicans* syn. *Echium fastuosum*) at The Nut in Stanley.

Milligania densiflora are found at high altitudes in Tasmania.

Orange fungi growing
in tarkine rainforest.

Manuka (*Leptospermum scoparium*) is a widespread shrubby species in Tasmania.

Horseshoe falls in Mount Field National Park.

Forest gum trees.

Trowutta Arch.

Green forest.

Cradle Mountain.

Apple orchard.

Vineyards in Tamar Valley.

Franklin River Nature Trail.

Russell Falls, Mount Field National Park.

Tropical forest in Mount Field National Park.

Horseshoe Falls.

West coast of Tasmania after heavy snowfall.

Blue river at Douglas Apsley National Park.

Enchanted forest with lush mossy plants and ferns.

Tulips Garden.

BEAUTIFUL & UNIQUE

New Norfolk and Derwent River.

Dairy and beef cows and bulls, organic and free range on a farm.

New Norfolk.

Dunnaley Bay and farmland, Dunnaley.

Bridestowe Lavender Estate.

Sunrise in country Tasmania.

Poppy field. Tasmania is the world's largest producer of licit alkaloid mater al, supplying almost half of the world's pharmaceutical demand.

Disused farming and stock shed.

Meadowbank Lake.

Alpacas.

Huon Valley highland longhair cattle farm.

Convict barracks ruins in Stanley.

Cradle Mountain reflected on Llake Dove. Cradle Mountain National Park.

Sheep farming.

Dairy Farm, Pyengana Valley.

Gordon River Road, Florentine.

Mount Roland.

St. Clair Lake.

Eucalyptus forest, view from lookout at Mount Field National Park.

RAILWAY
CROSSING
STOP ON RED SIGNAL
KEEP TRACKS CLEAR
KEEP LEFT

Ulverstone.

Richmond Town.

Morris General Store historic building in Swansea on the east coast of Tasmania.

Tamar Valley.

Mount Roland Regional Reserve and Olivers Road.

Coles Bay.

Tamar Valley.

Penny Royal Village.

Watermill and cottage in Penny Royal World.

Old Hobart Town Model Village, Richmond.

Strahan.

Colonial houses on Arthurs Circus, Hobart.

Tunnack.

Holy Trinity Anglican Church, Launceston.

Historic Evandale.

Beaconsfield.

Tasmanian Winery.

Deloraine.

Stanley.

Vineyard on Tasmania's north coast.

Fresh oysters by the sea.

Truffles.

Salmon fish farm.

Bread and cheese board.

Meat pie.

Foraging blackberries in the wild.

Apricot.

Maria Island located on the east coast of Tasmania.

Yachts Moored off Hobart.

Fog Bank.

River Derwent.

Elizabeth Street Pier in Hobart.

Racing yachts on the River Derwent.

Cape Hauy and Tasman Sea, Tasman National Park.

First published in 2024 by New Holland Publishers
Sydney

Level 1, 178 Fox Valley Road, Wahroonga, NSW 2076, Australia

newhollandpublishers.com

A record of this book is held at the National Library of Australia.

ISBN 9781760796624

Managing Director: Fiona Schultz
Designer: Andrew Davies
Production Director: Arlene Gippert
Printed in China

10 9 8 7 6 5 4 3 2 1

Keep up with New Holland Publishers:

NewHollandPublishers

@newhollandpublishers